WHAT DO WE TELL THE CHILDREN...

and ourselves ?

Join me, in a survival guide -
bringing back morality and mental health,
an antidote to the examples set…
to helplessness … don't give up yet.

These times are
serious
pathetic
frightening

I offer
awareness
camaraderie
humor
some things, **enlightening**

Dr. Wendy Satin Rapaport
Clinical Psychologist

Contributions: Artist Laura Waller; Poets - Kathleen Ellis, Ellen Goldsmith, Claire Millikin, Mark Raymond, Judy Kaber, Lois Anne. Eileen Hugo, Alice Haines; Activist Lisa Breheny - "Nourish Maine"; Foreword by Dr. Sanda Bernstein - psychoanalyst; and an essay by psychotherapist Marilyn Charwat.

Front cover photograph of watercolor painting by Laura Waller
Darkness Descends: The Political World after Helsinki, July 16,2018
Cover design by Holly Vanorse Spicer
Editing advice Ellen Goldsmith (I think she wishes I was a better listener)

FOREWARD

It is with great pleasure that I write this Foreward to Dr. Wendy Satin Rapaport's newest book, <u>What Do We Tell The Children</u>. Dr. Rapaport, a noted psychologist with a specialty in treating patients with diabetes and their families, has now written a chapbook that is more personal, closer to her heart. She has taken on the challenge many of us face today as we confront a world in which lies are rampant, in which the civility we once relied on to conduct our affairs seems to have disappeared. She does this by sharing her thoughts on how we can use psychological understanding to manage our emotions and those of our children in these difficult times. She describes techniques which can enable us to calm and soothe ourselves as well as prepare for action. But this book is not just about psychological insights. In her book Dr. Rapaport shares her wise, witty and also moving poetry with us, poetry which speaks to these same important issues. She also shares the poetry of her poet colleagues.

Dr. Rapaport is not just a practicing psychologist, professor, lecturer, and the author of four books. She is also a poet and a great believer in the power of expressing oneself through the writing process. She has long participated in a group of people who write poetry and share it with one another. Writing poetry for both pleasure and catharsis is important to Dr. Rapaport.

In her current book, Dr. Rapaport uses two of her passions to enlighten us and move us and entertain us. As a reader, we learn from and are comforted by all of her passions: her passion to teach people to better understand themselves and others and her passion to use "Good Enough" writing to express thoughts and emotions and to encourage others to try it too.

As many of us struggle to find a path through our distrust and anger and bewilderment and hopelessness, and as we try to find a course of action which will allow us to feel empowered without losing our empathy, I can strongly recommend that we read and reread Dr. Rapaport's poetry-filled book for information, and more importantly, for inspiration.

Sanda N. Bernstein, Psy.D
Psychologist

Claimer (not disclaimer) from the author: Sandy and I love each other and yet *all* she says about me is objectively true. She is my co-author of *Friendship Matters.*

WHAT DO WE TELL THE CHILDREN...
and ourselves?

TABLE OF CONTENTS

WAIT...DON'T CLOSE THE BOOK...THERE ARE FABULOUS **POETS** SHARING THEIR IDEAS *CLOTHED IN BEAUTIFUL WORDS*

Protect the Children

Walk these streets with me
the avenues of slander and bullying
led by the *Lord of the Flies*
muddying and destroying

Is there a grown up on these mean streets?

PROLOGUE

It's normal to ask the question, ***What do we tell the children?***
You might even ask the advice of a psychologist, who unfortunately is also suffering from PTSD *Post Trump Stress Disorder*, admittedly not my naming, but still my condition. I worry about the impact of lies, hate and the predilection for revenge from this presidency on all of us, and our children. First, as the grown ups and parents, we have to help ourselves be clear and free from the depression, pessimism, disenchantment, anger, helplessness, rage and frustration permeating our atmosphere. We can feel these feelings, but we and our children need to land on our feet in compassion and constructive works. We don't want to end up bored or helpless or cynical. We want to identify the chaos and create a healthy separation from it. If we don't, and we get lost in our rage or despondency, the evil wins out.

I write this as a "Citizen Psychologist." I care about how you feel and react and want you to have all the tools to make sense of things. Your mind, heart, and mood matter. Understanding psychology is central. This guide takes you through rage, recovery, and then urges you to join a resistance of sorts for the issues that touch you. At the end of reading this, I hope you feel understood, had a release, and gained a new perspective on how to contentedly and effectively go through your day. I also wish for you a lot of positive conversation and connection with your family and a group that identifies with changing the things that disturb you. My ambition is that you will find what you are *for,* not against and work hard to make these things happen. We cannot stay silent, be complacent, cowardly and complicit, like many in Congress.

Let's be *part of the solution.*

A Poem A Day...

I want to be an eco poet
a poem a day
might not protect
the environment
from corrosive speech

I want to clean these spiteful streets
from the top - down -
Words that taint and destroy
flood the land with acid rain
capsize souls, pollute our moral choice
Daily slander brings slime
decays our bridges

Let's clean these mean streets
remember civilization
and for goodness sake
Don't let your children read the President's tweets

Advice to Parents

President Trump is not a kids' show.
It is rated "R", Restricted.
Kids, do not watch unless there is an adult in the room

I don't know if the President
failed boy scout training.
but he failed the boy scouts
"courteous, friendly, cooperative, kind"
not bragging, slanderous, self centered
He is an example to teach us
what not to do
how to not get a merit badge

WHAT'S A PERSON TO DO

This guide is an **antidote for negativity.** It will be a little gloomy, but just for catharsis not as a *position statement.* And it will be fun. Okay, okay not fun exactly. I do insist on a smile or two from recognition of ourselves or the situations. The purpose for my writing and you reading this is to heal ourselves from these infuriating times. I hope you experience the rotating process of *recognizing, healing* and *preventing* further wounds through *awareness* and *knowledge* of how you *feel* - and then *respond* to things we can not control. Here is the *process*, ways to clear our own minds and then teach the same strategies to our children.

- **Ventilation** ("Let it go")

  This may include beginning each day with "Are u $#@&+ kidding me?" We need complaints, then lots of amnesty for our thoughts.

- **Naming** (Understanding and recognition)

  After hearing ourselves speak or after listening to others, we *identify* (name) and *respect* our feelings. We slow ourselves down and sit with the understanding. We feel things but postpone our *negative* or *reactive* behaviors since initial reactions shift with time and tolerance. We teach our children to do the same.

- **Anger** (A common response after provocation - indignation and hostility)

  Still better than depression, which is *anger turned inward* on ourselves, dangerous because others can't help us if they don't know how we feel. When we are angry, we can get help.

- **Empathy** and **Positivity** (*Applying* in order to *Change* an initial response)

  A challenge in these times and hence a very small section

- Some more **Anger**
- **Putting the hate back in the bottle**
- **Stand your ground,** the good kind

DON'T JUST SIT THERE...HAIKU

Billie Jean King, star
Ivanka Trump not so much
Courage... it's beautiful

MAKE AMERICA KIND, AGAIN

A five year old and his new baby brother
are never left alone, thanks to the enlightened mother*
She will teach him toleration for his mixed emotion
It's normal** to need and practice self control until you also feel devotion
*give me a break, father or parents didn't rhyme
**unless you are the president

UNDERSTANDING FAMILY DYNAMICS

Understanding what goes on in families is important because the head of our country is like a parent to us. We are influenced by his behavior many times a day due to our frequent exposure to the media.The abusive parent as well as the "head" of our country can have extremely negative effects on the *children* - on us and *our* children. Having this knowledge can inform and calm us, and then empower us. We see that he frequently encourages *one child* to take his side against the other child (magnifying red vs. blue or Fox vs.CNN news). Children fight each other because of a parent or leader's behavior, in this case purposeful and dangerous *favoritism* and *put downs* of one side. You know how Cain and Abel ended up. (Excuse the simplified and reductive version.) He is dangerously stoking the fire, creating chaos by playing upon our **fears,** and stirring up **hate** as a dangerous *coping* mechanism. (My doctoral dissertation was on humor as a coping mechanism. It's a much better choice.)

In a healthy family, the parents are "checks and balances" on each other, making sure the kids feel equally valued as they go through normal challenges such as managing *differing gifts,* sibling rivalry, etc. When there are problems with the adults, e.g. if one parent drinks too much or yells, or lies - the other parent (Hello Congress? Hello advisors? Hello Melania?) is there to back up and respect *all* the kids and insist the out of control parent take a look at himself or herself and sees the insecurity being instilled in the kids.

I Thought I Heard a Robin Sing

What a wonderful news release-
the world, at last, finally at peace.

Alas it's hard for one's own family
to create and sustain a harmony.
Believe me, it's them not me
who start the unending insanity.

So how on earth can we create
a world respectful, state by state?

So maybe it should begin with me -
reflect on anger...bring empathy.
Self respect can then unfold
Caring and interest unleash my bold
True wealth: the self, the family
please don't forget the community
and know the other, carefully

IN OUR FAMILIES, sometimes we find ourselves trying too hard, "walking on eggshells," trying to please the disturbed parent or leader. When we are functioning in a healthier manner, we know the alcoholism or abuse or craziness or vengeance or revenge **is not about us.** It is better to have a *boundary* - a shield- (and understanding) so the venom cannot pour over us, changing *our* moods or behavior.

 Daddy (excuse my chauvinism) is the problem, not us. L*et us separate from him* and not inherit *his* craziness, manipulation, fear mongering, homophobia, bigotry. *Let's not take his side. We must not let him "split" **us.*** We and "the base" need to know each other. With empathy, we have to understand the attraction and needs of the other so his "side" is satisfied by *real* security. We take a moment to understand the often unconscious attraction to the "Bad Boy." People who walk around feeling powerless and inadequate may be vicariously intrigued by the leader who has seemingly unlimited power, flaunts all rules, uses intimidation tactics, and shows uninhibited disrespect for many. Doing what he wants to women or in business, usually unacceptable impulses for most people to "actually" do, some supporters can find second hand pleasure in connecting to the person who does.

An insult a day
is the bully's way
not the American way

Let's stop the cultural divide
We will not let him split us up
should we be *right* or friends
We did the civil war already
No reruns. Lots of people died

United we stand, divided we fall

LOYALTY

The government runs on independent integrity (or it did)
Republicans - soul check
What would you tell your child who has a friend who steals?
Challenging *is l*oyalty

The *government* should be operating as a *family*, regarding each of the branches, which includes the free press, as equal and respected members. All of them should be challenging each other to do their best for the family, not just for themselves.

THE ENEMY OF THE PEOPLE

He actually said that
this time, about the free press
called them scum

pointed to the back of the room
I know he hoped the masses
would attack them

What happened to *We the people*
not red or blue
I'm good you're bad

He is the enemy of the *people*
I will love my brother
… red, white, and blue

The Man Who Would be King has
loyalty oaths signed to him,
not to America

Thank goodness for the fress press
so we know
who is the enemy of the people

KATHLEEN ELLIS is the reason I write poetry at all. She is the most gifted of professors at the University of Maine, or the university of anywhere. She is brilliant, stimulating, warm, inviting, and humorous. She will make you think, too. A version of the poem was published in *Cabildo Quarterly in 2013*.

32 REASONS FOR SURVEILLANCE

Our foes are in our midst and all about us.
—Henry David Thoreau

Someone knew someone recited the *Qu'ran* in her basement at night.

Someone knew someone borrowed sugar from a Muslim.

Someone told someone to mind her own business.

Someone told someone your business is my business.

Someone told someone she loved Omar Khyaman, a Taliban rap artist.

Someone saw a lady in a chartreuse dress kiss a cop in Boston after

watching a Pussy Riot video.

Someone never answered her cellphone & didn't tweet or text.

Someone swore someone on Facebook had stolen her image.

Someone swore someone had stolen her imagination.

Someone swore someone had stolen her name & numbers.

Someone swore someone wished to remain nameless.

Someone complained about America's infrastructure.

Someone complained about America's info structure.

Someone complained about America's statesmanship.

Someone complained about America's ship of state.

Someone complained about frost heaves on the back roads.

Someone complained about global warming.

Someone complained about colder weather.

Someone complained about lack of wilderness.

Someone complained about lack of courtesy.

Someone complained about too many acronyms.

Someone complained about acrimonious sales clerks.

Someone complained about illegal immigrants.

Someone complained about dog poop on the sidewalk.

Someone complained about cruelty in April.

Someone complained about taxes.

Someone complained about T.S. Eliot's wife.

Someone complained about the obscurity of poets.

Someone complained about the language of love.

Someone complained about the explication of the text.

Someone complained love & war were the same text.

Someone complained to somebody, and someone told somebody else.

—Kathleen Ellis

And there's no question you know them. But, stress brings out the need for the refresher course.

At Least, Do No Harm. We remind ourselves of what it takes to help our children - and us - on a good day. Now, more than ever we need *The Skills,* first for ourselves and then our children so that we can keep from being overwhelmed and pointed in a direction to do something positive.

You know the drill.
With all this hatred
We need more than good will

- Remaining ***Accepting, Curious*** and ***Interested*** in what our children (you get it, that includes us) feel, especially in times of today's brutality. We have to stop and ask questions, have conversations, never assuming that we or our children get over the daily assaults that can leave us devastated.

- ***Listening*** and ***Reflecting*** back to the person we are talking to so that we acknowledge that we hear the other person's meaning correctly, that we *understand* and *validate* how *they* arrived at their feelings. Validation does not necessarily mean we agree with them. If our children have different responses to things than we have, and we feel aghast, we must stay with kindness to see how they have arrived at their thoughts and feelings.

- Being fully invested in ***Emotional Literacy*** - awareness and self-regulation of our positive and difficult feelings.The process begins with stopping to acknowledge, respect, and have *compassion* for *our* feelings. Next we "reappraise" our perspective by *empathizing* - really understanding what the *other* person feels, as well, and why he acts a certain way. That's kind to them and us. And, it's a lot of work. Of course, there's more: practicing forgiveness and sharing gratitude. And, it's only 9:00 am. Begin again. It gets easier. Repetition builds the emotional literacy *muscle.* Just another workout.

- Understanding the need for healthy ***Boundaries*** - *separation* - from the contagion of others' negativity and rudeness. It is difficult to not be influenced by our environment unless we are *mindful* and *conscious* of "choosing" our response. *When they go low, we go high. (Michelle Obama.)*

- Cultivating "***Truth Literacy*",** using critical thinking and evaluation to weed out bias and opinion. This includes suspecting "sensational" ideas and checking out *confirmation bias,* the tendency to believe only ideas that agree with ours. Rejecting evidence takes us away from democracy, e.g.Trump is still talking about a witch hunt- he wishes- after 12 Russian hackers were arrested for *cyber* warfare.

- *Coping* and *thriving* through **humor, kindness, honesty**, and **friendship.**

- Cultivating ***Affirmations***, authentic and positive statements that are useful to helping us *soothe* ourselves when we feel wounded by negativity, whether directed to us or to others. The affirmations are truthful and add *perspective* to the situation, ruling out *all or nothing* thinking that we are learning from this presidency. What we say to ourselves dictates our moods. We make a point to recognize the angry and helpless "self-talk" - and purposefully substitute **authentic** and **positive** thoughts.
  Positive Affirmations:
    - About Oneself: *"I am strong and I will figure out a way to get past my helplessness. I know these feelings will pass.* That's kinder than "I am okay. You, not so much", though you can begin with that as a warm up.
    - About one's country: *America is great. Its leader is trouble.*
    - About all the friends and family members who disagree with your point of view, *My neighbor is a loving and wonderful person. I will like her, be kind to her - even though I am shocked by her personal views. I don't have to love her till the president's term is over. (Scratch that last line.)*

- ***Respecting Differences*** by wanting to really know and understand where people are coming from. If you are not shown the same thoughtfulness, affirm to yourself that you are okay, and they are not, in this instance. Step back and think about how their fear and anger is not about *you,* but about *their* insecurity.

- ***Giving*** and ***Receiving Compassionate*** and ***Constructive Criticism*** means that you can tolerate negatives that come at you without being crushed. When it is your turn to answer, you will always begin with honest kindness rather than rejection or hostility. When you wish to *give* criticism, begin with the same compassion and perspective - nuance - too, e.g. *You are always such a careful, thoughtful and honest person.* ***I wonder*** *why you don't seem to question the hatred and negativity of the King* (I don't mean Elvis) or be bothered by his lying, *gaslighting* us to only believe what he says rather than what we read or see. Keep the positive and put it in perspective; begin with *I like...*

- Application of ***Resilience***, promoting our personal assets to predictably respond in a deliberate - rather than reactive - manner to setbacks and challenges. It moves us away from holding grudges and being preoccupied with revenge.

(Seriously, this is tough stuff for all of us. How do we become parents without getting training and a license? But then that's another dissertation.)

WHAT DO WE TELL THE CHILDREN WHEN *WE SEE* WHAT THEY ARE SEEING

WE NEED A SYLLABUS. We have a leader who is a "role model for **sins"** that we warn our children to **avoid**, including the sin of disinterest, denial, and indignity. Our kids are watching, listening. ***What do we tell the children?*** We have to make sure they do not copy what they are watching. We have to talk more to them to ask them what they see and the kind of person *they* want to be.

It's painful to see his *public **defiance*** of the ***Golden Rule or 10 Commandments:***

Blasphemy: The modern and secular extension of blasphemy, accompanied by poetic license, is the maligning, contempt and "irreverence" for humanity that we see in his bullying, compulsive cyberbullying - "Bully Mania". Unfortunately, every day social media *unleashes* the repressed bully in all of us, like a contagion. Hopefully you don't find an increased rudeness in yourself, but if you do, reign it in because you don't want to become what you don't like.

Bearing false witness: Yes, that's about lying. Deliberate falsehoods are different from "projection" - an *unconscious* defense mechanism wherein a person doesn't wish to know or own their own unacceptable qualities and attributes them to another. If we listen carefully to a person who uses this, we can see what is really on *his* mind, e.g. the labeling of fake news is what **he** is doing. When it is *consciously* done, as a *tactic*, it is no longer about coping but purposeful malicious lying to plant doubt in ourselves and the *other.* (gaslighting), e.g.Crooked Hillary or is it Crooked Donald?... What happened to prosecuting *slander*?!!!!

> The lying insults and humiliating shakedowns, verbal abuse, intimidation, and unpredictability are sometimes followed by a warm handshake. It is a pattern imitating ***intimate partner violence.*** (This comparison does not minimize the danger and damage of those actual situations.) It is difficult, frightening, controlling and confusing for the leader's *victims* and *us,* the *spectators,* experiencing *vicarious trauma.* It can keep us overwhelmed.
>
> For some people following him, it's ***identification with the aggressor,*** a symbiosis for survival and safety by following the aggressive parent, the one with caveman power. I suppose that in part, some supporters may be feeling that he is *for* them - but really the connection is only based on loss, fear and hate. He is not going to *leave them out*...of the hate. A wonderful wake up call for all of us is to think "inclusion", but not on angst and loathing.

The Ten Commandments, Violated...continued

Adultery: Need I say more, *#Me too,* wish the country would say more. *I apologize*, his start, *fired*, our finish.

Stealing: Including Melania's version of Michelle's talk, without *her* follow through.

Murder: Seriously in Charlottesville the administration's equivalence of sides that murder and those that don't. For our sanity, we need a clear condemnation.

Covet thy neighbor: Kim and Kanye and Trump, worshipping the golden calf.

WHAT DO WE TELL OUR CHILDREN WHEN *WE SEE* WHAT THEY ARE SEEING

JUST SAY NO! to these violations of civilization.

Let's hope this works and they don't play *Follow the Leader.*

Atonement...he didn't win the popular vote...even with the hacking
Victory when he acknowledges he won ... assisted by Russia's backing

And if you find that **JUST say NO** is not enough and they begin to *copy...*

Would you ground your child who has broken these rules?

Hear me roar
Watch me smirk
I'm a stable genius
it stems from my shoe size
and *I don't care* if you lost your shoes
or your parents in the separation
Hate crimes are up
alongside shame for being who we are

Would you ground your child who has broken these rules?

They are watching and listening carefully
How do you stop your children
from becoming,
worshipping the tools
of ugliness and danger...
unbecoming

The good news
They have been immersed
in a course about personality and *mental illness.*
Take a knee
knowledge gives us power
Or license

Grandiosity the religiosity of the self
the presidency should not be run by oneself
all the facts he will rearrange
from what is truth to climate change

We must teach, with the most respect and empathy for the painful origins of this behavior in patients, family, friends, ourselves, or our leaders. *We* can do this, because as people and mental health providers, *we* are determined to have *self regulation over our impulses.* That's emotional literacy at its finest. But when someone has *unchecked* and unregulated impulses, it causes pain to others. The despair inflicted on the person and their family and our country can be helped, when recognized and treated, rather than acted out each day.

I wish we could say *You're fired.* I think I will go put on the TV. At least with *Madam Secretary,* she works it out.

GETTING A GRIP ON ABNORMAL AND DANGEROUS BEHAVIOR

Note: These are illness *observations,* not a diagnosis of our president.
If we understand and "see" what's going on, we can separate ourselves from the drama, have *boundaries,* and not be drawn in. We can create *proactive* reactions in ourselves, and prevent becoming caught up in the downward web.

- **Personality issues,** from genetic, brain, social or environmental factors, can result in unstable feelings of worth and rocky relationships. Oftentimes, when a perceived slight occurs, the person can seemingly flip into a rage. At this time, they might *split* their emotions - having neither nuance or patience - and think they or others are good and the rest of the world is bad. As impulse control can be a problem, the person might be prone to say or do something. A more *well adjusted* person can work through these feelings or thoughts and would "Think, before you speak", just like our mothers taught us.
  E.g."Lock her up" (Seriously, in America, without due process?)
  E.g. Trudeau warmly hugged then disparaged, while Putin and Kim are seen as *remarkable.* After he puts down our allies, he sides with Putin the dictator over our FBI.
  E.g.Women should be punished for their abortions.

- We have seen patterns of **abnormal behavior,** narcissism, in inflated feelings of importance, an excessive need for admiration, power and success. Further we can see an addictive drive to bully for personal satisfaction, i.e. thriving on strife and chaos to come out as hero.
  E.g. *No one is smarter than me.* I bask in the applause and I will do anything to get it
  E.g. I brag and bully people
  E.g. I disparage someone daily; my satisfaction and ego comes from creating disruption and then swooping in to talk about how I will save the day, e.g impulsive chinese tariffs ending up with subsidies to farmers. Hey, what about the Maine fisherman?

- A pattern of **antisocial** attitudes and behavior with no apparent empathy or conscience, resulting in no inhibition about taking advantage of people.
  E.g.Separating parents from their children
  E.g.Being in no hurry to reunite them
  E.g.Blackmailing the families: they will get their children back if they don't seek asylum.

PTSD from the President

We are reeling…
"Moral equivalency",
daring to compare
two things
not the same,
is taking us down…
in action and feeling.

Nepotism
Let your children take over positions unsuited to their experience.

The klu klux klan has good people.
Please say you are kidding.

Obsequious self criticism…
America is not so perfect…"We are all to blame" referring to Russian *meddling* in elections…honoring Putin and himself over our own government-perverted witticism

Separation of children from their parents.

Meddling, the inaccurate diminutive; it is, in fact, *information warfare,* an act of war.

We must heal
Fight the *misinformed (*Sigh, what strides from *ill informed). Can you say lied to?*
And shout
Find clout

We must fight for justice and equality.
Get up.
We can't stay stunned.
Silence will take us backwards.

Find 10 people to vote...who agree to find 10 people to vote …

a *good* Pyramid Scheme

HANDLE THE STRESS OF POLARIZATION

One of the things we must consider in life is how to listen. It helps us to expand our original thoughts while holding onto ourselves. Opening our minds only means broadening ourselves to more than *our* guts and intellect. In a writers group, you actually ask for feedback and incorporate the groups' thoughts. It makes us see through many lenses, enables us to handle constructive criticism, reminds us to have empathy beyond ourselves and still maintain an excellent sense of self, even better than when we started.

I recommend writing. My first book of poetry was called "On the Couch with the *Good Enough* Poet, how writing turned an average neurotic into an average poet." Writing is not only for the talented. It's a way to learn what you know. And you don't have to be good at it, just *good enough*.

I recommend writing in a group. It's community, challenge, and continued thinking. That's how we get a piece of the PIE (Passion, Interest, Empathy and Equilibrium).

HOW WRITING POETRY IN A WRITERS GROUP MAKES ME A BETTER AMERICAN

It's the epitome

of free speech
Ideas I didn't know

become in reach

Of course I like
applause
Instead my gifted friends

cause me pause

They know I really want the praise
instead
make me reappraise

and so I grow
from what I do - and don't know

They like me...They really really like me

Try it, if you can
It makes you a more thoughtful American

CH -CH -CHANGE

Women's rights were meant to be about gain. We have to step back and think about the "other", that it may feel more like loss of status or opportunity for men, at first and maybe for a while. As comedian Sebastian Maniscalco kiddingly says, "The man cave *was* the *entire* house." Now, he just might have a room. Important that we recognize and have empathy for people during the "process" of adjustment. Clearly, most people have a little trouble, *normal* human adjustment, with new ideas and rules. The women's movement, affirmative action, LGBT rights, the true end of racism, health care and immigration, will be good for everyone, at some point. Good change doesn't always make everyone equally satisfied and can be uncomfortable, at first. Patience and tolerance - without changing our goals - can *not* be in short supply. My husband Jim says we should keep being kind, regardless of what we get in return. He is wonderfully under the influence of the Mr. Rogers documentary, "Won't you be my neighbor. "

Friendship is so valuable. It helps us make changes. I want you to hear the thoughts of my beloved Marilyn Charwat who is a prominent psychotherapist. You are lucky to listen to her or go to her professionally for the "cure." Her whole life has been involved in activism, in particular women's rights, insisting us into consciousness and action. She says:

In nature there is only growth... and decay. Nothing else. There is no middle ground .
We can see the decay eating away at our culture now. The only way we can save our culture is to change. The only change that is possible is to change aspects of our culture that are suffering, incorrect or ignored. We have to address that or the disparate areas will bring the culture down. We work on the things...for all of us.

When evolution was taking place, homosapiens were divided into two directions, one peaceful and semi communal and the other savage and violent. The savage and violent group won and continues to evolve into current day homosapiens. What saves our culture are the ideas that evolved alongside such as cooperation, group and tribal support, religious ideas of spiritualism, kindness, community, and caring. With those we survive as a culture. Much of the humanizing part of our culture is from women and selfless containment, translating into bigger ideas. Without this, we die. With these, we go on and support each other into a culture of contentment, equality, personal and global growth, and love.

Change, it'll do me good

CHANGE

They say to *reset* - rearrange
our thinking and our smiles
I don't want to. It hurts
Chicago or bust...Go west young man
I am all curled up. I don't like dirt
Sigh. Too many untravelled miles
I rearrange and ch- ch- ch- change....*It'll do me good*

SERIOUSLY

The Supreme Court
Meets the baker and the love birds
Discrimination to individuals
That takes the cake

Presidential Pardon
Please say "Excuse me
I'm Leaving"
I will not beg your pardon

The definition of Paranoia...
The CIA
and the FBI
are not trustworthy

SO WHAT'S REALLY NEW?

I had freckles, a really big smile and the atom bomb
I remember when we practiced hiding under the desks.
In retrospect, a lot of good that would do.

In ninth grade, during the Cuban missile crisis
the boys wanted to save us from dying as virgins.
In retrospect, a lot of good that would do, for them

And now that awful feeling, again, of going to the brink
You'd think they would have developed diplomacy along with hydrogen
In retrospect, a lot of good that would do.

"Kids, this too shall pass. Go outside and play..."(Oh, you don't do that anymore?)
Put down your phone and love a friend or neighbor as you would have them love you.
A lot of good that *would* do.

REFLECTIONS: IN SEARCH OF HEALING

WAKA DIPLOMACY

Waka is classic Japanese poetry…
twice the lines and perhaps twice
the pleasure of Haiku

our side of the story

is still one sided

the North Koreans (and Republicans) eat , pray, love - too

See me, feel me, touch me, heal me...

political correctness is correct, you know

it means we have made a human connection

we see the whites of their eyes,

we fire our recognition

from inside out

A day passes in the life of PTSD...

Did I Say Healing

When hearts are faltering

(and they should be rising)

the leader of no feeling

women's rights are leaving

split families grieving

racism thriving

How are we surviving?

Hope

Get out the vote

Be a candidate

Write poetry

Sign petitions

March...that's your ammunition

Evil wins when good people do nothing Albert Einstein

Here's a prose poem from my editor in chief, a dear friend, terrific poet, and excellent poetry professor, **Ellen Goldsmith** who pushes us to **shake ourselves up and listen**, to the other, and have appreciation for **how *great* America already is**, in spite of our leaders. We always need **perspective,** it's not all or nothing.

Walden

was the homework for my evening class at a community college where I was pretty new and the students came to class tired from a hard day's work, tired but they did the reading and I was tired too because my house was being painted and I felt weighted down by too many coffee table photography books and more dishes than I could ever use so after the inspirational "Only that day dawns to which we are awake" I read quotes like "A man is rich in proportion to the number of things which he can afford to let alone" and "...my greatest skill has been to want but little" and I had more, but you know how you can feel people leaving the room even though they're there, how their bodies empty out and everything that makes them vital recedes beyond the back wall. So I stopped with my quotes and asked what was going on and after some silence one man said something like, "Lady, you may feel weighed down by stuff but we don't have a lot, we want more, doubles, triples even" and then it was my time to be silent and the silence was like a border between some kind of not knowing and knowing and it isn't that I was completely unaware that different life experiences lead to different views but I learned more that night than I learned from my multiple readings of Walden and I try to carry it with me but just now it's hard, hard for me to stay in the room, hard to ask why as a genuine inquiry as I did in my class that night because the people in my country elected a President I think unfit, even dangerous (although I remain grateful that I feel safe writing the word dangerous).

Ellen Goldsmith

Published in PenBay Pilot May 22,2018

A Change: Heart and Mind

*American Sentences...*Allen Ginsberg's gift
           the "new haiku"
           17 syllables...compact observations with emotion

1. If only the first words you said had loving kindness. It's good to dream.
2. The soft-spoken poet laureate made a big bang. I heard him smile.
3. The fears of the hurricane blew into the wind as I watched *Big Bang.*
4. If women would rule the world, if we'd go down, we'd do it caringly.
5. It wanted to be clearing. You knew the sun was pushing its way lightly.
6. **Say Yes.** My mother rolls over in her grave. It's fine Mom, it's a good yes.
7. Green eggs and fried clams. Dr. Seuss, New England special, roll over ham.

In Praise

What America means to me
I liked our fourth grade assignment
when things were clear
runny nose, not distinguished by allergies, colds, or contagion
straightforward and factual, our praise
immigration and resilience
opportunity and optimism
with liberty and justice for all

In praise of America
In praise, no kidding, one person at a time

One of the challenges in life is to stay rooted in liking ourselves, *not taking in* prejudice. We must guard against allowing insults or discrimination to contaminate us. Hate is about the *other's* discomfort, not about who you actually are. As Mr. Rogers said, *I like you just the way you are.* (Were you waiting for a quote from Freud?)

Integrity

Coursing through their bodies
stream full-bodied emotions
love and anger
desire and rage
fear and wisdom

welcomed or not
ready or not
here they come

prepared for plantation policy
subjugation...surveillance
Their hands are over their ears
They let you spew

Even if they earn 75 cents on the dollar
and you have a double standard for their performance
they will not be forgotten
or overlooked

They will resent but still perform
and lock arms
and kneel but not to the master
in solidarity with their sisters and brothers

They let out a big sigh
commit to kindness and benevolence
and continue to enjoy
integrity

EXHORTING

1. SAY WHAT?

People chat about *happiness*
An unstoppable grin, a ready laugh
The gait, a skip, the generosity rampant

Who could remember? I am sour and mad
Like a mad dog growling
Don't mess with me, I feel ruthless
    Nothing a short hospitalization, homicidal watch, couldn't cure
    If the president is willing to go

2. OPERATION CHANGE IT UP

My husband says, *Stop complaining*
I yell back at him, shocked he isn't as angry as I am
You're a child of the 60's, he says
Why do you let daily ranting on racism, homophobia, xenophobia, anti-Semitism,
compulsive lying, women's rights
    from the top…
    get you down?
I hear him and go to the broom closet
get out my walking stick, dust off the cobwebs,
stop flying off the handle, no witch hunt.

I light my fire, ask *you* to be *for* something, too… get a plan, get active.

RETURN TO AMERICAN VALUES AGAIN Haiku

Separation of church
and state does not mean
separation of children from their families

AND NOW

we owe reunification
of the bodies

and *healing*
of their hearts
and minds
>   Their mantra...the families are courageous, brave
>   In the midst of America's mistake

and ours, who are
wounded in the watching
and replenished in the marching

REFRAINS
>   (Wish he would refrain)

It's huge
The likes of which you've never seen
President Obama did it
I have a good relationship, a great relationship

>   Ahh ode to originality and thoughtfulness
>   and the end of slander
>   the beginning of humility

It's an aberration
overnight sensation
on the cliff of damnation
We will not be pulled in
to live in the sin
of counter-revolution
with similar pollution

So we open our eyes
decide to stay wise
think compromise
on the details not the values
And we will continue to see
that you are a lot like me
We'll effort to be free

Which means we will listen
in order to be heard

It's fascinating, the steadfast way people hold onto their views. If the clinging is to important values, like goodness or justice, it's admirable. On the other hand, it's dangerous when "confirmation bias" or "my side" bias doesn't allow for processing new information objectively, unfortunately faithful to "belief perseverance", regardless of the fresh information presented.

I suppose none of us like to be "wrong"
I just wish we could enjoy being "right", *now.*
Find pride in changing course.

DEAR KIDS (and ourselves)

Don't become what you don't like
the dissonance will drown you
Don our life vests
and stop the "cruelty to kids" policy
at the borders, with our guns

Love thy neighbor
Feed the poor
Drive people to the polls
Hand out mail-in ballots
     Love all thy neighbors

Make it better
Help the downtrodden

Understand and forgive the hateful
Tolerate the haters
That needs two sentences

Watch the "FAKE " news
which stands for *free*, *actual*, *correct* and *enduring*
which is keeping America great
"All hands on deck"

WE ALL HAVE A POINT OF VIEW

So *he* hears you
respects you
and
we do the same
maybe to agree to differ
but to see
how we are the same
and
how we might "lean" in
stop
being the"other"
for each other

It's base
to talk about someone's
base
They stop being people
who we see

We must make connection
be inclusive
not divisive
find the energy
to transcend the struggle
(so we might snuggle)
take a bath together, in empathy

Stop the labeling.
It stops us from seeing
and brings us to judging.
As Eckhart Tolle says…
When you tell a child the name of a bird,
he no longer sees the bird in the original way.
He sees the name

WHAT WE TELL OUR CHILDREN

Know right from wrong
> which is turning out to be right and left if I absorb the
> personality of our fearful and dark leader

Listen, Reflect
> *Speak up*
> *Speak out*

Do not give up
> Shout until you are *blue*
> in the face and the heart

Encourage *others* to *join* you
Don't make *assumptions* about race or money or politics
> unless you *judge to the good*
> in the face and the heart

Have *gratitude.* See your full cup
> And when you fall, take a moment, then *get up* :)

Don't be *changed* by evil
Have *Courage...*Be *Civil*
Hold hands, *Connect*
Surround yourself with goodness
> It keeps us in check

Think beyond yourself
Caring, altruism, and competency - your wealth
Think before you speak. Self control is not overrated
> Even though this phrase is rather dated. Thanks momma

Honor your *individuality.* Stay *true* to THE *truth*
> "Happy is the man who has not followed the counsel of the wicked"

Your security comes from *your* thoughts and actions
Bear witness. "Keep on trucking" in *righteousness*
***Tikkun olam* (repair the world), there's power in your youth**

WHAT *WE TELL* THE CHILDREN!

WE HAVE BEEN BEATEN UP....
dazed
We must rise
from the fall
from destruction
and disruption

Here's the ending
or the **beginning** of this story...
the kids grieve
and thank goodness,
They *stand their ground*...the good kind

ISN'T IT GREAT...
The KIDS*
are telling
US

*Parkland

DON'T PUT THE BOOK DOWN. STAY AND HEAR *OTHER* POETS
WHOM I CHERISH AS PEOPLE AND POETS

CONTRIBUTIONS FROM PHENOMENAL POETS

Claire Millikin has so many talents and gifts, probably the most intellectual and down to earth person and professor I know. Her poetry, just one of them...

Hearts and Souls

Hearing my husband's voice on waking that November morning,
the morning after, *It's over,* I felt my heart was failing.
Running five miles that afternoon
with every step, a new unsteadiness of pulse.

Was it possible, do hearts really fail from dread?
Heart and soul move entwined
as water in all its manifestations— ice, thirst, sky.

The night before the election, I dreamed he won
and became wealthier in office by selling luxury condominiums
in the arctic circle, so the rich could watch the ice
melt, as the ocean rose higher and higher, eustacy,
and the poor drowned in uncurbed global warming.

He sold the pleasure of watching
ice melt as ocean dissolved into steam, watching
as those desperate without money drowned,
while the rich stayed safe in their luxury condominiums
in the arctic circle. And when I awoke my heart went cold:

there's no building that can keep the soul
in the end, every action returns.
Hearts and Souls, the old song,
what goes around comes around.
Hearts and Souls, in a different key, return--

Claire Millikin

These are profound thoughts by **Mark Raymond** a poet who teaches at James Madison University. Thank goodness for his clarity, intelligence and good nature.

In the comedy *Sleeper* by Woody Allen (another guy who we have to talk about what to tell the kids), a man cryogenically frozen in 1973 reawakens to a dystopian America 200 years in the future. One scene early in the film involves a scientist questioning Allen's character, a typical wisecracking nebbish, about some artifacts from the distant past. Showing a video clip Richard Nixon, the white-coated scientist explains that, while they theorize the man had been a U.S. President, all records of him have been "wiped out"—"there's nothing in the history books . . ."

I think often these days about the ephemera of the Trump presidency—how, for instance, those souvenir pencils and placemats that display our presidents' heads in chronological order will never not include #45. Since Trump's face is nearest the eraser end of the pencil you don't even get the pleasure of grinding him up straight off to get back to a nice sharp point at Obama. For the future, for the kids, Trump's record will never be wiped out—his face will always be there, smiling just like Nixon's, along with Jefferson and Lincoln, Carter and Reagan, Martin Van Buren and Rutherford B. Hayes.

I was a kid when *Sleeper* came out. America's cultural response to the Watergate scandal was in high gear, although at the time I probably understood the specifics as well as I got the off-color sex jokes in Allen's film—they were like artifacts from an adult present that you made sense of distantly, imperfectly. The radio played novelty songs about the scandal ("Haldeman, Ehrlichman, Mitchell and Dean/Things won't be the same when we're gone from the scene . . ."). Stores sold reams of paperbacks (one cover showed a caricature of Nixon's head, his nose a running faucet, an allusion that seemed right to me as a kid with the news awash with references to leaks, White House Plumbers, and Watergate). An older cousin's teenage bedroom, swinging in full-blown counter-culture, included a naked cartoon Nixon light switch cover—just picture the switch you turned on and off as Dick.

For today's kids as well, what lasts in their psyches will be impressions made by the potsherds and dejecta of our time, the souvenirs, novelties and jokes, as transient as Snapchat and archived with question marks and asterisks, exclamation points and hashtags, notes upon those mystic writing pads that you can't really wipe out.

It's kids like Barron that I worry about. What's it going to be like growing up under the shadowy record of your dad's monstrosities? Himmler's daughter just died, loyal to the end. It'll take generations, three or four at least . . . and then, what America will they awake to?

Still, look at Ronan Farrow and the good work he's been doing.

Counting the Night
(November 9, 2016)

Maybe the sun won't come out. Times have seen

longer yesterdays—dark endless hours, home to prophets

who spat to the future, leopards couched in the temple

ready to lap up the spill. We've heard there's nothing left

before, dry curses on dashed rocks, old songs

to hold our tongues in strange lands. Revelations

make no sense. Redactors get their word in. Tribes rebel.

Again, nothing happens that someone didn't see.

Already, somewhere, someone's counting on the night

like a thief, ready to be woke in a strongman's house.

Mark Raymond

Judy Kaber is an incredible poet. This poem is powerful and graphic and reminds us that the

separation on the borders may have the kids thinking *they* have done something wrong to

deserve this. And, there's no telling how much of their lives will be changed, going forward.

In Solitary at Fourteen

Days held prisoner in this awful space, minutes spent
pacing, gulping air, a fitful chalky blue. The way

sultry August slid beside me each night, I miss that
strut stuff, trying always to hit the beat, tune

in the tenor of the streets, out among the devils and demon
howls of city. Here my ears bite on moans, clanking steel,

invisible inmates with bitter nuts and bolts touching
my pain. I want to drain my cells, start over, tell my brother

he don't know squat. But what I did, I did. No games here.
Not one place where I can make a cheap hit, blast zombies

til they all drop and sleep with the controller on my chest.
One mat, toilet, sink. Nothing to do, nothing to think until

the day comes I stand before the judge. Well, I got no child
left in me now. Don't know about after. Not dark enough

and I can't sleep.

        Judy Kaber

Lois Anne is a talented artist who eagerly took on the banner of writing poetry, a star again...

NOVEMBER 9, 2016

George Orwell came to visit last night
Scaring the shit out of me
Not because he was a ghost
But because he said "I told you so."

SUGGESTIONS

What do I tell the children?
And anyone else who asks?

Read Ursula Hegi
"Stones From the River" first
Then "Children and Fire"

Look around you
And think ...

Read George Orwell
"Animal Farm"
And "1984"

Look around you
And think ...
And weep

And, lastly, in the words of Joe Hill
"Don't waste any time mourning.
Organize!!"

                    Lois Anne

No Poet Goes Gentle Into the Good Night

when pain is all around

Practicing mindfulness, I put my phone away and begin to talk to the cashier at the market. He seems surprised, that I'm asking him about himself. He says most people ignore him, that they are snooty about the working class, he doesn't matter. When I exclaim, *Of course not. They are addicted to their phones or preoccupied or in a hurry. It's not about you.* He isn't buying it. He's steeped in his prejudice about their presumed prejudice.

No poet goes gentle into the good night. I have work to do.

Please don't eat the prejudice
and please don't assume it's everywhere
(Remember the popular vote)

I love that I look Jewish
I won't flinch
unless you are armed
with hate or ammunition
I'll still love that I look Jewish
and I may turn the other cheek
so you won't see the tears ...
not about me, but for the fear you live with
and how you use hate to bring you comfort

I will not join you in your dislike
and I will not dislike you for your dislike
I don't put bitterness in my tea
though it is tempting when I am not disciplined
to sip on the poisons of prejudice
Rage. Rage against the dying   of empathy

Eileen Hugo is a wonderful poet. Retired now, she keeps on writing superb things. Thank goodness she is not really retired.

Weiwei Says *The world is a sphere, there is no East or West.*

Picture the world from space

clouds swirling over a blue orb

east and west do not exist

humanity and inclusion coat

the edges of continents

the edges of peace

Listen To Me

I struggle to explain that lying isn't ok
my children old enough to listen to the news
he says fake news   implies the news is a lie
he says she is a liar   but gives her money
contradictions pile up against truths
you must seek the truth and celebrate it
check your facts   stand up for justice

Eileen Hugo

Alice Haines is a physician who spent three months as a medical volunteer in Dadaab Refugee Camp on the Somali border. Her lyric poetry often features the natural world and interpersonal and intercultural work experiences.

Refugee Camp Refrain

What did you have for breakfast
green pea soup
What did you have for lunch
green pea soup
What did you have for dinner
green pea soup
What did you do all night
green pea soup
-Anonymous
children's game.

What overflows the pit latrines
pea-green soup
Who's got mouths that need to eat
thirteen million children
Where do you get your oil and salt
distribution trucks
Why don't you get a different home
your greed *our* luck

What did you have for breakfast
corn meal mush
What do you have for lunch
nothing much
What do you eat for dinner
questions why
What do you do all night
hope to fly

Alice Haines

It is not easy to go from "grumbler" to activist, but hoping this reading helps push you in that direction. **Lisa Breheny** is a wonderful activist who has done many things in the Rockland community but whose latest project is "Nourish Maine"

The power of light
Reach to the heights of the source
Within
Without
Where will you be this day
Carry it to the night.

Nourish Maine is an organization promoting empowerment of individual and family lives. We aim to partner children and adults with chefs (professional and home cooks) to prepare nutritionally balanced and healthy meals for $3.00 or less per person.

We are filing for 501(c)3 status and plan to begin the project in 2019.

Our hope is to bring this program fully to all 50 states.

If you would like to contribute to this essential program, please make donations payable to:

NourishMaine
c/o Paul Gibbons, Esq.
PO Box 616
Camden, ME 04843

Many thanks in advance, Lisa Breheny
NourishMaine@gmail.com
If you are able to contribute and you have done so because of reading this book, just say so and let them know Wendy will match 10 % of your gift.